Down the Field

10, 20, 30

A Football Counting by Tens Book

by Martha E. H. Rustad

AMICUS READERS 1 AMICUS INK

Say Hello to Amicus Readers.

You'll find our helpful dog, Amicus, chasing a ball—to let you know the reading level of a book.

1

Learn to Read

High frequency words and close photo-text matches introduce familiar topics and provide ample support for brand new readers.

2

Read Independently

Some repetition is mixed with varied sentence structures and a select amount of new vocabulary words are introduced with text and photo support.

3

Read to Know More

Interesting facts and engaging art and photos give fluent readers fun books both for reading practice and to learn about new topics.

Amicus Readers and Amicus Ink are imprints of Amicus
P.O. Box 1329, Mankato, MN 56002
www.amicuspublishing.us

Library of Congress Cataloging-in-Publication Data

Names: Rustad, Martha E. H. (Martha Elizabeth Hillman), 1975- author.
Title: Down the field 10, 20, 30 : a football counting by tens book / by Martha E. H. Rustad.
Description: Mankato, MN : Amicus Readers, 2017. | Series: 1, 2, 3 count with me | Includes bibliographical references and index.
Identifiers: LCCN 2015041446 (print) | LCCN 2016015632 (ebook) | ISBN 9781607539216 (library binding : alk. paper) | ISBN 9781681521121 (pbk. : alk. paper) | ISBN 9781681510453 (eBook)
Subjects: LCSH: Counting--Juvenile literature. | Football--Juvenile literature.
Classification: LCC QA113 .R889 2017 (print) | LCC QA113 (ebook) | DDC 513.2/11--dc23
LC record available at https://lccn.loc.gov/2015041446

Photo Credits: Corbis/David Madison, cover, Zach Bolinger/Icon SMI, 4; Getty/Ryan McVay, 20, 24; iStock/Willard, cover, Charles Mann, cover, dehooks, 6-7, 24, AndreyPopov, 8, 24, pidjoe, 10, 11, bbostjan, 10, 11, BaMiNi, 10, 11, Nastco, 10, 11, ZargonDesign, 12, Atid Kiattisaksiri, 15, 4x6, 16, DustyPixel, 18, 24; Shutterstock/Danny E Hooks, 1, Aspen Photo, 3, Ulrich Mueller, 6-7, antpkr, 16-17, Joe Belanger, 18-19, 24, Joseph Sohm, 22-23

Editor   Rebecca Glaser
Designer   Tracy Myers

Printed in the United States of America

HC 10 9 8 7 6 5 4 3 2 1
PB 10 9 8 7 6 5 4 3 2 1

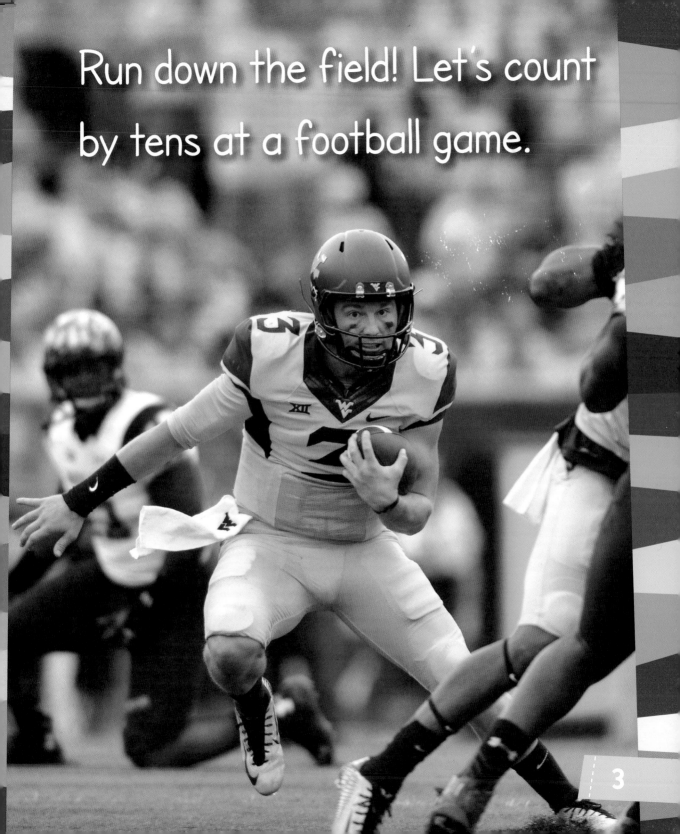

Run down the field! Let's count by tens at a football game.

quarterback

10

Ten players huddle around the quarterback. He calls out a play.

Twenty players set their helmets in the locker room. A helmet protects a player's head.

30

Thirty cheerleaders clap and shout. They lead fans to cheer. Yeah!

40

Forty pairs of football shoes have spikes for extra grip.

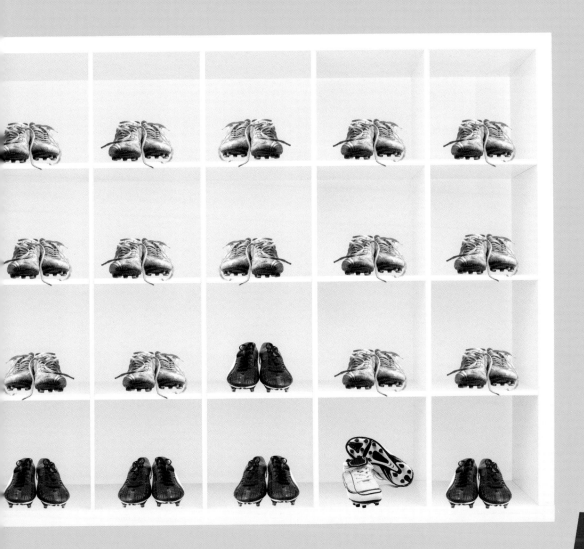

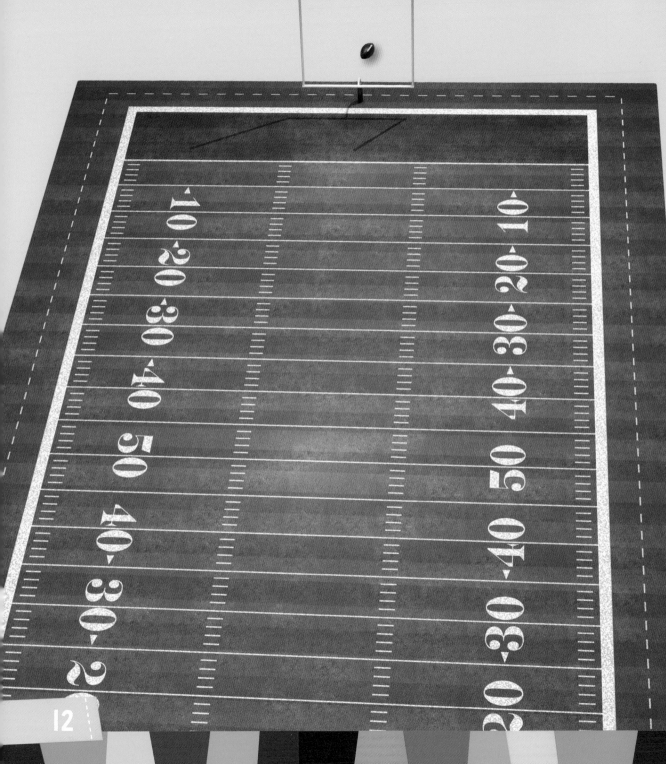

50

The kicker kicks the ball fifty yards. He scores a field goal. Three points!

60

Sixty yellow seats are empty after the fans leave.

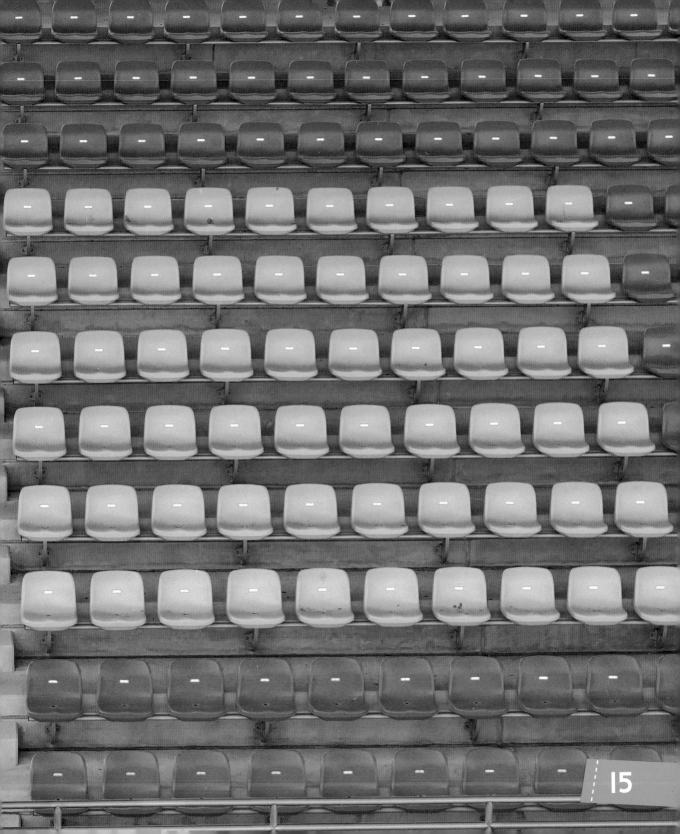

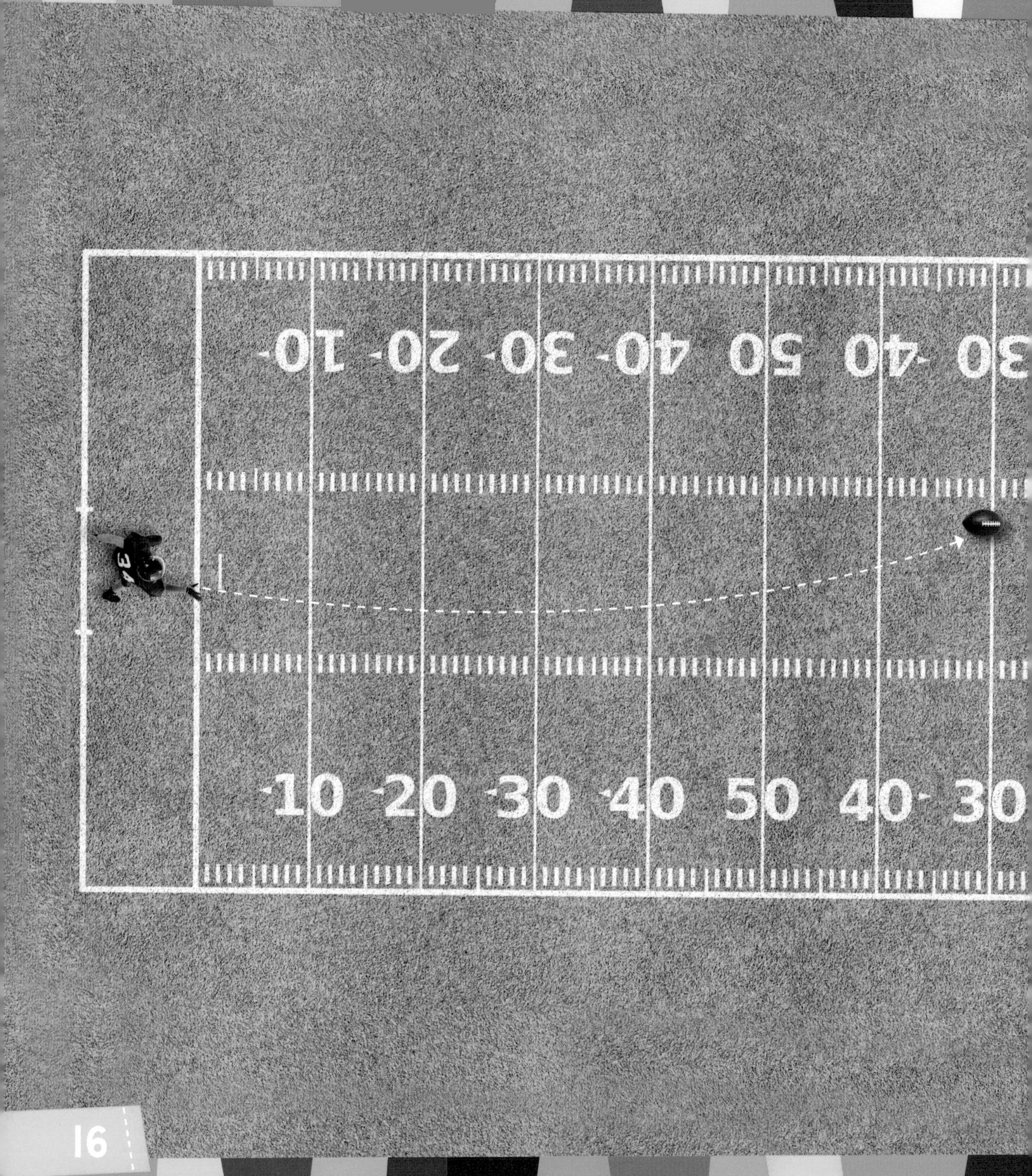
10 20 30 40 50 40 30
34

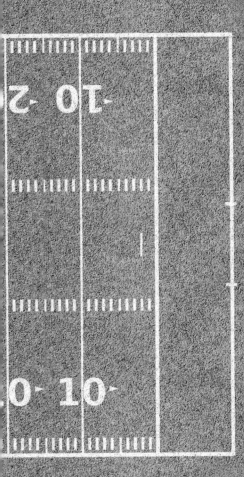

70

The quarterback throws the football seventy yards. A player catches it. Then he drops it. Oops!

Eighty hot dogs cook on grills. Hungry fans tailgate in the parking lot.

80

90

Ninety band members play at halftime. The third quarter is about to begin.

100

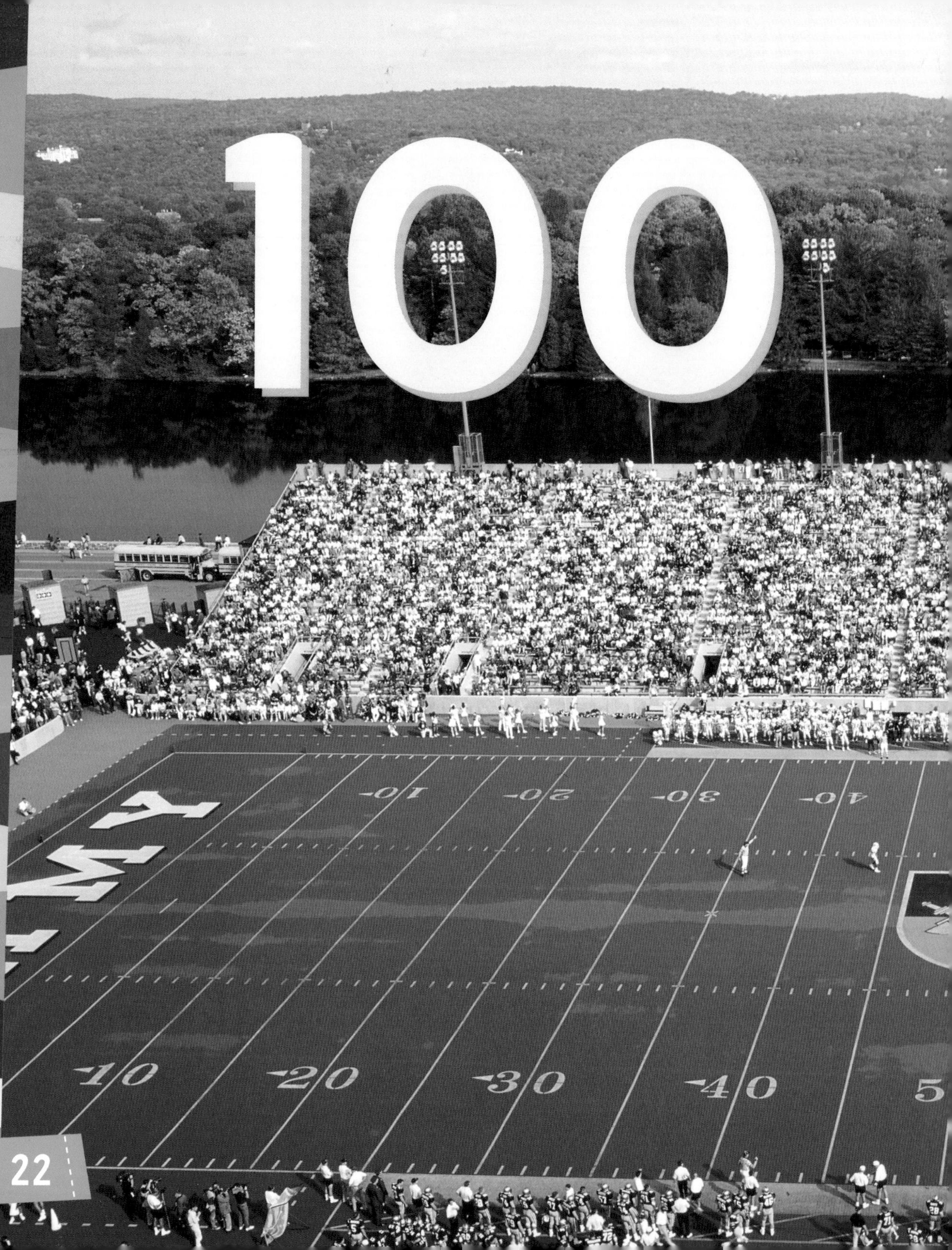

A football field is 100 yards long. The teams are ready to play. Hike!

Count Again

Count the objects in each box by tens.

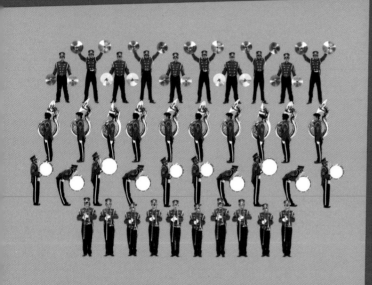